Cool & Creamy

The Ice Cream and Frozen Yogurt Book

Gay Hendricks
Carol Leavenworth

A SPECTRUM BOOK

PRENTICE-HALL, INC., Englewood Cliffs, New Jersey 07632

Library of Congress Cataloging in Publication Data

Hendricks, Gay.
    Cool and creamy.

    (The Creative cooking series) (A Spectrum Book)

    1. Ice cream ices, etc.   2. Yogurt, Frozen.
I. Leavenworth, Carol, joint author.   II. Title.
III. Series.
TX795.H53   641.8'63   79-10940
ISBN 0-13-171975-0
ISBN 0-13-171967-X pbk.

10 9 8 7 6 5 4 3 2 1

Printed in the United States of America

Editorial/production supervision by Shirley Covington
Interior design by Jeannette Jacobs
Cover design by Al Pisano
Interior art by Joyce Biegelieisen
Manufacturing buyer: Cathie Lenard

Prentice-Hall International, Inc., London
Prentice-Hall of Australia Pty. Limited, Sydney
Prentice-Hall of Canada, Ltd., Toronto
Prentice-Hall of India Private Limited, New Delhi
Prentice-Hall of Japan, Inc., Tokyo
Prentice-Hall of Southeast Asia Pte. Ltd., Singapore
Whitehall Books Limited, Wellington, New Zealand

Contents

The Creative Cooking Series

Every recipe in each of our cookbooks has been kitchen tested by the author.

BOOKS IN THE CREATIVE COOKING SERIES

Preface

**Homemade ice cream. Fresh, pure & simple.
And now the zesty newcomer, frozen yogurt.**

Not only do these words make the taste buds hum in antici-
pation, but they also bring happy pictures to the mind: spring
and summer, Sunday afternoons, days gone by, beaches,
childhood, good times and tastes.

For those who take the little bit of time necessary to make
homemade ice cream and frozen yogurt, rich rewards will
come in the form of compliments, sound nutrition, and great
tastes. In this book you will find recipes that are good for you
as well as being good to the taste. As we, the authors, tried
out these recipes, we found to our delight that the simplest
recipes with the freshest, most natural ingredients were the
ones that got the most passionate raves from our family,
friends, and neighbors. If you have a gourmet touch, though,
you need not despair: there are many exotic recipes in the
book on which you can try out your skills.

Are homemade ice cream and frozen yogurt good for you?
Absolutely. If you go easy on the sweeteners, as we have done
in this book, you have a natural food made of dairy products
and pure flavorings. Dairy products are a good source of
protein and are one of the basic foods recommended to be
part of our daily diet. By varying the ingredients, you can
make the recipes outrageously rich for an occasional treat, or
airy and light for daily consumption. Perhaps the best testi-
monial we can give to the nutritional virtue of homemade ice

v

cream and frozen yogurt is a personal one. During the time we were working on this book, we ate a lot of ice cream and frozen yogurt (to say the least!). We both felt great, and we both lost weight.

It is not necessary to be a gifted cook to make good ice cream and frozen yogurt. Your authors are merely passionate amateurs. Our idea of a gourmet meal is hot homemade bread, a hearty soup, and a bowl of our own ice cream. Our desire to keep things simple has led us to include, for example, several different ways to make vanilla ice cream, each with a slightly different twist. Occasionally, though, we let our imaginations run wild to come up with some of the farther-out recipes later in the book.

We, the authors, are psychologists by profession. You may wonder how we became interested in writing a book about homemade frozen desserts. One reason is our belief that simple, lovingly prepared food is nourishing to the spirit as well as to the body. Making high-quality things to eat is good therapy for those who make it and those who eat it. Further, we would like to see adults and children become fond of healthful desserts rather than the sugary, soulless things to which many are addicted. Then, too, we are lifelong lovers of good ice cream and recent zealous converts to frozen yogurt, and we enjoy sharing the recipes we have discovered over the years.*

We found much pleasure in making and eating the cool and creamy treats in the pages that follow. We wish you the best of luck in the delicious journey ahead.

*We would be delighted to have you look at some of our other books on psychology and education. You particularly might enjoy **How to Love Every Minute of Your Life** and **The Centering Book** (both Prentice-Hall).

How to make your own homemade ice cream

In making your own ice cream and frozen yogurt, you have several ways to choose from. The three most popular ways are the hand-cranked churn freezer, the electric churn freezer, and the type of machine that goes inside the freezer compartment of your refrigerator. Let us discuss this latter gadget, then talk about churn freezers.

There are various makes of inside-the-freezer machines available. The one we tried and found satisfactory is made by Salton and retails for about $25. There is another brand which works approximately the same way but which sells, believe it or not, for $625. It is great for status (Danny Kaye and a few other Hollywood types own them), but we doubt that the ice cream it makes is $600 better.

The way this machine works is that you put the ice cream or frozen yogurt mix in an inner container, insert the churn, then pop on a lid that has an electric motor in it. You then stick the whole works in the freezer, run out the cord and plug it in, and shut the freezer door. Presto! In an hour or two you have a quart of frozen dessert.

We recommend this type of machine, although we found the texture of the dessert to be somewhat airier than when made with the standard ice-and-salt churn freezer. It eliminates the

3

potential mess of ice and salt, and is good for people in a hurry. One hint on using the Salton machine. The inner container has a plastic lid with a hole in the top. Due to heavy use and repeated changes in temperature, this lid will probably break, as ours did after a week or two of use. We found that the plastic lid from a three-pound can of coffee was exactly the same size. We got one, cut a small hole in it, and have been using it ever since. Your alternative is to buy a new lid from the Salton factory.

Now to consider churn freezers. This is our favorite way to make ice cream and frozen yogurt. Although purists will shudder, we prefer the electric model. You get the same special taste as you do with the hand-cranked model, but without all that cranking! The churn freezer, invented by an American woman around the middle of the nineteenth century, works like this. You put alternate layers of ice and rock salt about two-thirds of the way up the side of the freezing container. You add your mix, put in the churn, cap it, and crank. The rapidly melting ice freezes the mix as the churn aerates it and causes an even distribution of ice crystals. Sooner than you think, you have a luscious dessert.

A standard size is the model that holds two quarts. Most of our recipes in this book are designed to make a quart of dessert in a two quart freezer.

Keep it clean
Your equipment needs to be scrupulously clean. Even if you washed it carefully before you put it away last time, wash it again before you start this time. Remember also to wash all the salty brine out of the ice bucket. You may want to keep a big bowl of water around while you are making ice cream to rinse things in quickly.

4

Ice

Get a good supply of ice. For the two-quart size freezer, you will need two five-pound bags of cracked ice, or enough to fill the bucket of the freezer without the freezing container in it. Ice cubes do not work as well as cracked ice. So put your cubes in a heavy plastic or burlap bag and bash them until they are cracked ice.

Salt

Rock salt is the kind to get. In the winter it is used for melting ice on driveways. In the summer it is sold (sometimes at twice the price) for making ice cream. You will need one cup of rock salt for making ice cream in a two-quart freezer. If you get the late-night munchies and have no rock salt on hand, you can use ordinary table salt, but cut back to about two-thirds of a cup.

The mix

Be sure to chill the mix before putting it in the freezing container. If you don't chill the mix, the resulting dessert will be of a different texture than the best ice cream ought to be. Between one and two hours of chilling will be fine. Some of the recipes have gelatin in them, however, so do not chill these over an hour.

The sweeteners

We have used a variety of sweeteners in the recipes. We use raw sugar and honey more than anything else, but we urge you to experiment to see what suits your taste. Our tendency is to avoid refined sugar when possible; with some recipes, though, it is the sweetener that works best.

5

Putting it all together

When you pour the mix into the freezing container, only fill it up two-thirds of the way. This will leave room for it to expand as it becomes ice cream.

Assemble the machine. Make sure the lid is on tight. Before adding salt and ice, crank it a few times or plug it in to see if everything is working properly.

Now put in three layers of ice and salt. Notice where the drain hole is on the side of the bucket. Put in a layer of ice that comes about a third of the way up to the hole. Sprinkle a third of the salt evenly over the ice. Then repeat the procedure twice more, so that you end up with ice about the level of the drain hole. Then pour a cup of cold water evenly over the salt-ice combination. This should cause the level to drop. You may then add more ice up to near the top of the freezing container.

Now you are ready to freeze. Plug the machine in or get a contingent of crankers ready. It will take about a half-hour to freeze, less if you are hand-cranking. It is ready when it becomes hard to crank or when the motor sounds like it is suffering unbearably. Another way to tell is to peek and see if the mix is piling up around the shaft of the churn.

If you like a harder ice cream, and if you are masterfully patient, you can then take the churn out and let the mix set for a while in the bucket or in your refrigerator's freezer to achieve a harder consistency. If you are like we are, though, you will eat it while it is still soft. Actually we do not do this only out of greed and impatience; in our opinion, softer ice cream has a better flavor. See what you think.

6

What can go wrong

Although ice cream is quite easy to make, several things can go awry. Fortunately most of them can be repaired.

Salty brine can get into the mix. This usually happens when someone peeks carelessly or when the lid is not put on snugly. To avoid this tragedy, make sure to sponge off the moisture from around the lid when you peek. Many of the freezers nowadays have clear plastic lids that you can peek through without lifting. If you should spill some brine in the ice cream, quickly grab a big spoon and dip out the top few inches of ice cream. Chances are the brine will not have had time to spread throughout the mix.

The mix might freeze too fast. This usually happens when the mix is too thick, especially with frozen yogurt. If you suspect this is the case, thin out the mix by adding a little milk. Another reason for too-fast freezing is that you have put in too much salt, causing the ice to melt so fast that the ice cream freezes to the side of the can. If this happens, scrape the ice cream away from the side of the can, add some ice, and try again.

Your mix might not freeze. The simplest thing to do is to put in another layer of ice and salt. If nothing happens, you can doctor the mix. Take it out, reheat it, and add some softened gelatin. Or put in two beaten egg whites. Chill the mix and try again.

It is very likely, though, that none of these things will happen, and you will make superb ice cream the first and every time.

7

Ice cream

2

Philadelphia vanilla

When many people remember what ice cream used to taste like, this recipe is what they are thinking of. It is simple and pure. This type of vanilla ice cream is called Philadelphia Vanilla because of the Philadelphians' lovely custom of including the seeds and pulp of the vanilla bean in the ice cream.

    1 cup heavy cream
    2 cups half-and-half
2/3 cup of sugar*
    1 split vanilla bean
       pinch of salt

Step 1
Put half of each cream in the top of a double boiler, along with the sugar, vanilla bean, and salt. Cook over low heat, stirring constantly, for 10-15 minutes, or until slightly thickened. Remove the pod of the vanilla bean, but leave the seeds and pulp.

Step 2
Chill the mixture.

Step 3
After chilling, mix in the rest of the cream. Churn.

11 *Natural foods folks can use raw sugar here, but do not use honey in this recipe in particular, and in vanilla ice cream in general. The taste of honey is so strong that it overpowers the light, delicate flavor of the vanilla.

Vanilla
à la Française

3/4 cup evaporated milk
1/2 cup sugar
    pinch salt

  4 egg yolks

  2 cups whipping cream
  1 tablespoon vanilla

Step 1
Heat milk in top of double boiler and stir in sugar and salt until dissolved.

Step 2
Beat egg yolks until foamy. Add a small amount of hot mixture to egg yolks. Combine egg yolks with evaporated milk mixture, stirring constantly over hot water until mixture begins to thicken. Cool.

Step 3
Combine cream and vanilla with cooled milk and egg mixture. Chill two hours and churn.

This recipe is simple but exquisitely rich. The egg yolks give the ice cream a depth and texture that is memorable. If you desire a lighter variation, substitute half-and-half for the heavy cream.

Frozen vanilla custard

1 cup whipping cream
1/2 cup sugar
    pinch salt

3 eggs, well beaten

2 cups creamed cottage cheese
2 tablespoons vanilla
1/4 teaspoon nutmeg

Step 1
Combine cream, sugar, and salt in top of double boiler and heat, stirring constantly until sugar and salt are dissolved.

Step 2
Add small amount of warm mixture to beaten eggs. Then slowly add eggs to warm mixture, stirring constantly until mixture begins to thicken. Cool.

Step 3
Combine cheese, vanilla, and nutmeg in blender until smooth. Add to cooled mixture. Chill two hours and churn.

13

Traditional chocolate ice cream

3 tablespoons cocoa
3/4 cup sugar
1/2 cup evaporated milk
1 tablespoon unflavored gelatin, softened

2 cups whipping cream
1 teaspoon vanilla

Step 1

Combine cocoa and sugar in top of double boiler. Slowly add evaporated milk, stirring constantly to avoid lumps. Heat and add softened gelatin, stirring until dissolved. Cool.

Step 2

Combine cream and vanilla with cooled mixture. Chill one hour and churn.

This recipe combines the traditional "back to the basics" flavor of chocolate with a deep, velvety texture. You will lose count of the sighs of pleasure this ice cream will bring.

14

Butterscotch ice cream

1/3 cup butter, melted
2/3 cup brown sugar

1/2 cup evaporated milk
  1 teaspoon unflavored gelatin, softened
    pinch salt

  2 cups whipping cream
  1 tablespoon vanilla

Step 1
Combine butter and brown sugar in top of double boiler and mix well until sugar is dissolved.

Step 2
Add milk, gelatin, and salt to butter and sugar mixture and heat, stirring constantly, until gelatin is dissolved. Cool.

Step 3
Combine cream and vanilla with cooled mixture. Chill one hour and churn.

A good butterscotch ice cream does something mysterious to the taste buds: it begins with a burst of lightness but ends with a lingering, haunting aftertaste. Eat this one slowly to savor the complex interplay of flavors.

Mexican chocolate ice cream

2 squares unsweetened chocolate
1/2 cup evaporated milk

1 tablespoon unflavored gelatin, softened
2/3 cup sugar

2 cups whipping cream
1/2 cup whole milk
1 teaspoon ground cinnamon

Step 1
Combine chocolate and evaporated milk in top of double boiler until chocolate is melted.

Step 2
Stir gelatin and sugar into hot mixture until they are completely dissolved. Cool.

Step 3
Add cream, whole milk, and cinnamon to cooled mixture, chill one hour and churn.

On several trips to Mexico over the last few years, we discovered and learned to love our neighbors' custom of combining the flavors of chocolate and cinnamon. The Mexicans eat their chocolate and cinnamon largely in the form of candy bars and custards. We were unable to find an ice cream with this combination in any of the myriad ice cream parlors we visited, so we decided to make one of our own.

Easy chocolate mint ice cream

2 cups whipping cream
1 cup half-and-half
2/3 cup chocolate syrup
1/4 cup sugar
1/4 cup white creme de menthe or peppermint schnapps
  pinch salt

Combine all ingredients in top of double boiler. Heat, stirring constantly, for five minutes. Chill mixture two hours and churn.

Whoever first combined the flavors of chocolate and mint ought to get the ice cream equivalent of the Nobel Prize. The cool and breezy taste of mint is a perfect complement to chocolate. Here we have added the boldness of liqueur, but if you want to make a teetotal version, a few drops of mint flavoring can be substituted.

Chocolate mint chip

1/2 cup half-and-half
 2 teaspoons unflavored gelatin, softened
2/3 cup sugar

 2 cups whipping cream
1/3 cup crushed minted chocolate
1/2 teaspoon mint flavoring
2-3 drops green food coloring, if desired

Step 1
Heat half-and-half in top of double boiler. Add sugar and gelatin, stirring constantly until dissolved. Cool.

Step 2
Combine remaining ingredients and add to cooled mixture. Chill one hour and churn.

Make a trip to the candy store and buy a handful of chocolate mints. Refrigerate them for a while, then crush them up. Sprinkled throughout this rich recipe, they make a crunchy, stunning ice cream.

Mocha almond fudge

2 tablespoons instant coffee crystals
2 tablespoons cocoa
2/3 cup sugar
1 cup half-and-half

2 cups whipping cream
1/2 cup slivered almonds

1/2 cup fudge topping

Step 1
Combine coffee, cocoa, and sugar in top of double boiler. Slowly add half-and-half, stirring constantly to avoid lumps. Heat until sugar is completely dissolved. Cool.

Step 2
Combine cream and almonds with cooled mixture. Chill two hours and churn.

Step 3
Swirl fudge topping in as soon as churning is complete.

19

Mocha chocolate chip

2 squares unsweetened chocolate

1/2 cup evaporated milk
1 1/2 teaspoon unflavored gelatin, softened

3 tablespoons instant coffee crystals
3/4 cup sugar

2 cups whipping cream
1 teaspoon vanilla
1/2 cup crushed chocolate chips

Step 1
Melt chocolate in top of double boiler.

Step 2
Add milk slowly to melted chocolate in top of double boiler. Heat, and stir in softened gelatin until dissolved.

Step 3
Mix sugar and coffee together and add a small amount of milk mixture, mixing well to avoid lumps. Add to warm mixture in double boiler and heat, stirring constantly, for five minutes. Cool.

Step 4
Combine cream, vanilla, and chocolate chips with cooled mixture. Chill one hour and churn.

Easy fresh strawberry crème

```
    1  cup light cream
    2  cups whipping cream
    1  cup fresh strawberries, crushed or chopped
2/3   cup sugar
    1  teaspoon vanilla
       pinch salt
```

Combine ingredients, chill two hours and churn.

Fresh and pure, with just enough sweetener to bring out the natural flavor of the berries. And you can make this delicious ice cream in less than ten minutes. If you substitute honey for the sugar, use only half a cup. You will get the sweetness without overwhelming the berries.

Raspberry
ice cream

1/2 cup half-and-half
2/3 cup sugar
  2 teaspoons unflavored gelatin, softened
    pinch salt

  2 cups whipping cream
3/4 cup pureed raspberries
1/2 teaspoon vanilla or almond extract

Step 1
Heat half-and-half in top of double boiler. Add sugar, gelatin, and salt, stirring constantly until dissolved. Cool.

Step 2
Combine remaining ingredients with cooled mixture. Chill one hour and churn.

Your favorite berries may be substituted for raspberries in this recipe.

Peachy-keen ice cream

1/2 cup evaporated milk
2/3 cup sugar
    pinch salt

  2 egg yolks

  2 cups whipping cream
2/3 cup fresh peaches, finely chopped

Step 1
Heat evaporated milk in top of double boiler. Add sugar and salt, stirring constantly until dissolved.

Step 2
Beat egg yolks until foamy. Add a small amount of milk mixture to yolks. Then combine yolks with warm mixture, stirring constantly until mixture begins to thicken. Cool.

Step 3
Combine cream and peaches with cooled mixture. Chill two hours and churn.

With fresh fruit ice cream, our usual tendency is to keep it light. Here, though, we found that the egg yolks build a solid foundation under the ethereal peaches to make a most satisfying dessert.

23

Brown sugar cinnamon ice cream

2 cups whipping cream
1 cup whole milk
2 egg yolks, beaten until thick and yellow

1/2 cup brown sugar
1 tablespoon cinnamon
1/2 teaspoon vanilla

Step 1
Scald 1 cup cream and milk in top of double boiler. Add a small amount of hot mixture to egg yolk; then combine with ingredients in double boiler. Continue cooking, stirring constantly, until mixture begins to thicken. Cool.

Step 2
Mix remaining cream, sugar, cinnamon, and vanilla until sugar is completely dissolved. Combine with cooled mixture. Chill two hours and churn.

We love cinnamon and think it is underused in making homemade ice cream. Try this recipe to top off a light meal.

French chocolate chip ice cream

1/2 cup evaporated milk
  2 egg yolks
2/3 cup sugar
1/8 teaspoon salt

  2 cups whipping cream
  1 tablespoon vanilla
1/2 cup shaved, chipped or crumbled milk or dark chocolate.

Step 1
Heat milk in top of double boiler. Beat together egg yolks, sugar, and salt. Add to evaporated milk and cook, stirring constantly, until mixture thickens slightly. Do not boil. Cool.

Step 2
Combine cream, vanilla, and chocolate with cooled egg mixture. Chill two hours and churn.

We developed this combination of flavors one lazy afternoon when a family poll resulted in French vanilla and chocolate chip ice cream receiving an equal number of votes. The result of the stalemate has become a family favorite.

25

Rocky road ice cream

2 squares unsweetened chocolate
1/2 cup half-and-half
3/4 cup sugar
pinch salt

2 cups whipping cream
1/3 cup finely chopped walnuts
3/4 cup miniature marshmallows

Step 1
Combine half-and-half and chocolate in top of double boiler and heat until chocolate is melted. Add sugar and salt, stirring constantly until dissolved. Cool.

Step 2
Add cream and walnuts to cooled mixture. Chill two hours and churn.

Step 3
Stir in marshmallows immediately when churning is complete. Freeze.

This recipe is a children's favorite that combines the flavor of chocolate with the surprise of marshmallow and nuts. This dessert benefits from an hour in the freezer after adding the marshmallows; this allows for a greater contrast between the various textures.

Coconut punch
ice cream

1/2 cup evaporated milk
1/2 cup coconut liqueur
1/3 cup sugar
  2 tablespoons unflavored gelatin, softened
    pinch salt

  2 cups whipping cream
1/2 cup flaked coconut

Step 1

Heat milk and liqueur in top of double boiler. Add sugar, gelatin, and salt. Continue heating, stirring constantly, for ten minutes. Cool.

Step 2

Combine cream and coconut with cooled mixture. Chill one hour and churn.

This is a rich, tropical concoction with a mild alcoholic zing to it.

Mom's apple ice cream

3/4 cup sugar
1/2 cup water
1 cup finely chopped apples, peeled and cored
2 tablespoons brown sugar
1/2 tablespoon cinnamon
pinch salt

2 cups whipping cream
1 tablespoon vanilla

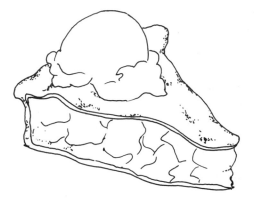

Step 1
Bring water and sugar to a boil. Add apples and cook until tender. Stir in cinnamon, salt, and brown sugar. Cool.

Step 2
Combine cream and vanilla with cooled apple mixture. Chill two hours and churn.

For a doubly delicious treat, try a scoop or two of this ice cream on a slice of hot, fresh apple pie.

Black walnut ice cream

1/2 cup evaporated milk
2/3 cup brown sugar
1-1/2 teaspoons unflavored gelatin, softened
    pinch salt

  2 cups whipping cream
1/2 cup black walnuts, finely chopped

Step 1

Combine milk, sugar, gelatin, and salt in top of double boiler and heat, stirring constantly, until sugar and gelatin are completely dissolved. Cool.

Step 2

Add cream and walnuts to cooled mixture. Chill one hour and churn.

There are some people who cannot get enough of walnuts. If you or someone you know is a walnut fancier, try this recipe. The brown sugar, with its light molasses flavor, enhances the taste of the nuts.

Malted milk
ice cream

1/4 cup malted milk powder
1/2 cup sugar
    pinch salt
  1 cup half-and-half

1-1/2 teaspoons unflavored gelatin, softened

    2 cups whipping cream
    2 tablespoons vanilla

Step 1
Blend malted milk powder, sugar, and salt in top of double boiler. Gradually add 1/2 cup half-and-half, stirring constantly to avoid lumps. Heat.

Step 2
Add gelatin to heated mixture and stir constantly until dissolved. Cool.

Step 3
Combine remaining half-and-half, cream, and vanilla with cooled mixture. Chill one hour and churn.

For Chocolate Malted Milk Ice Cream, add 3 tablespoons cocoa to malted milk powder and sugar mixture. Reduce vanilla by 1 tablespoon.

Honey cinnamon ice cream

1 cup half-and-half
1/2 cup honey
   pinch salt

2 cups whipping cream
1 teaspoon vanilla
2 tablespoons ground cinnamon

Step 1
Heat half-and-half, honey, and salt, stirring constantly, for five minutes. Cool.

Step 2
Add cream, vanilla, and cinnamon to cooled mixture. Chill two hours and churn.

A simple, natural masterpiece. Honey, vanilla, and cinnamon are good partners, and when frozen together into ice cream, they rejoice in each other.

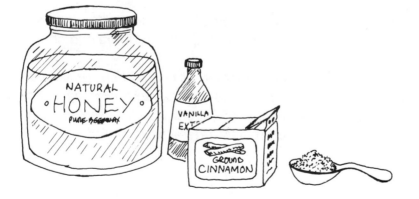

31

Cherry cheesecake ice cream

6 oz. softened cream cheese
1 cup whole milk

1-1/2 cups half-and-half
1/2 teaspoon almond extract
1 10-oz. jar cherry preserves
pinch salt

Step 1
Combine and blend cream cheese and milk with fork until smooth.

Step 2
Add half-and-half, almond extract, cherry preserves, and salt to cream cheese mixture. Mix well. Chill two hours and churn.

We made this recipe one afternoon. It was so rich we skipped dinner, and still were not too hungry the next morning. It has such a luscious combination of flavors that it deserves to be eaten slowly—maybe even with a demitasse spoon!

Marco Polo
ice cream

3 cups whipping cream
2/3 cup sugar
1 tablespoon vanilla
1 tablespoon cinnamon
1 teaspoon cloves
1/4 teaspoon nutmeg

Combine all ingredients, stirring until sugar is completely dissolved. Chill two hours and churn.

On his way to the East, Mr. Polo discovered many new spices. Here is a recipe that uses some of his findings to marvelous advantage.

33

Gimme Samoa ice cream

3 tablespoons cocoa
2/3 cup sugar
   pinch salt
1/2 cup half-and-half

2 cups whipping cream
1 ripe banana, crushed
1 teaspoon lemon juice
1/4 cup flaked coconut
1/2 teaspoon vanilla

Step 1

Mix cocoa, salt, and sugar until well blended. Slowly add half-and-half, stirring constantly to avoid lumps. Heat in top of double boiler until sugar is dissolved and ingredients are thoroughly combined. Cool.

Step 2

Mix remaining ingredients together and combine with cooled mixture. Chill two hours and churn.

Forgive the pun, but this tropical treat had everyone asking for some more.

Christmas ice cream

2-1/2 cups whipping cream
  1/2 cup sugar

  1/2 cup candied mixed fruit
    1 teaspoon vanilla
  1/4 teaspoon ginger
  1/4 teaspoon mace
  1/4 teaspoon cinnamon

Step 1
Mix cream and sugar together until sugar is dissolved.

Step 2
Separate fruit pieces and add with remaining ingredients to cream mixture. Chill two hours and churn.

It is high time for a new tradition—holiday ice creams. This recipe, blending the flavors of several spices and mixed fruits, will add old-fashioned elegance to any holiday meal.

35

Pistachio ice cream

3 egg yolks
2/3 cup sugar

1 cup half-and-half
pinch salt

2 cups whipping cream
1/3 cup finely chopped pistachio nuts
1 tablespoon vanilla
2-3 drops green food coloring, if desired

Step 1
Beat egg yolks with sugar until thick and yellow.

Step 2
Combine half-and-half and salt with egg mixture. Heat in top of double boiler, stirring constantly, until mixture begins to thicken. Cool.

Step 3
Combine cream, nuts, vanilla, and coloring with cooled mixture. Chill two hours and churn.

Try this recipe and learn what real pistachio ice cream tastes like. It is free of any artificial flavoring; you'll be surprised at the subtle flavors imparted by the vanilla and pistachio nuts.

Peppermint candy ice cream

   1 cup half-and-half
2-1/2 cups whipping cream
   1/3 cup sugar
   1 tablespoon vanilla
     pinch salt

   1/2 cup finely crushed peppermint sticks
   1-2 drops red food coloring, if desired

Step 1
Combine half-and-half, cream, sugar, vanilla, and salt, and stir gently until sugar is completely dissolved.

Step 2
Add peppermint and food coloring. Chill two hours and churn.

A fine vanilla ice cream with bursts of crunchy peppermint, this is the perfect treat for a summer evening.

37

Blueberry ice cream

3/4 cup fresh blueberries
1 tablespoon lemon juice
1/2 cup honey

2 tablespoons unflavored gelatin, softened

2 cups whipping cream
1/2 teaspoon vanilla

Step 1
Combine blueberries, lemon juice, and honey over low heat, stirring constantly until saucy.

Step 2
Add gelatin to blueberries and continue heating, stirring constantly, until dissolved. Cool.

Step 3
Combine cream and vanilla with berry mixture. Chill one hour and churn.

Try the recipe once this way, then make it again without cooking the blueberries. It makes two totally different tastes, both delicious but each with its own characteristics.

Coffee toffee ice cream

1/3 cup triple strength brewed coffee
1/2 cup sugar
  2 teaspoons unflavored gelatin, softened
    pinch salt

2-1/2 cups whipping cream
  1/3 cup crushed toffee candy
  1/2 teaspoon vanilla

Step 1
Heat coffee in top of double boiler. Add sugar, gelatin, and salt, stirring constantly until dissolved. Cool.

Step 2
Combine cream, toffee, and vanilla with cooled mixture. Chill one hour and churn.

This ice cream is for a day when you are not counting calories. It will satisfy any sweet tooth. For the crushed toffee, try Heath Bars. They are just the right flavor and texture for this recipe.

39

Maple nut ice cream

2 egg yolks
1/3 cup raw sugar

3/4 cup half-and-half
1/3 cup pure maple sugar
    pinch salt

2 cups whipping cream
1/2 cup chopped walnuts
1/4 teaspoon maple flavoring

Step 1
Beat egg yolks and raw sugar together until thick and yellow.

Step 2
Combine half-and-half, maple sugar, and salt with egg yolk mixture and heat in top of double boiler, stirring constantly, until mixture begins to thicken. Cool.

Step 3
Combine cream, walnuts, and maple flavoring with cooled mixture. Chill two hours and churn.

Cherry almond ice cream

1/2 cup half-and-half
1/2 cup sugar
1-1/2 teaspoons unflavored gelatin, softened
    pinch salt

2 cups whipping cream
1/2 cup fresh Bing cherries, chopped fine
1/4 cup slivered almonds
1/2 teaspoon vanilla
1/2 teaspoon almond extract

Step 1
Heat half-and-half in top of double boiler. Add sugar, gelatin, and salt, stirring constantly until dissolved. Cool.

Step 2
Combine remaining ingredients and add to cooled mixture. Chill one hour and churn.

Cherries and almonds are two delicate flavors that enhance each other magnificently. Here they combine with a rich ice cream to make one of our favorite recipes.

41

Louisiana bayou praline cream

2 egg yolks
2 tablespoons melted butter
2/3 cup brown sugar or maple sugar (use maple flavoring with
   brown sugar)

1/2 cup evaporated milk

2 cups whipping cream
1/2 cup whole milk
1/2 cup pecans, chopped

Step 1
Beat egg yolks, butter, and sugar together until thick and yellow.

Step 2
Continue beating while adding evaporated milk. Heat in double boiler, stirring constantly, for five minutes. Cool.

Step 3
Add cream, whole milk, and pecans to cooled mixture. Chill two hours. Churn.

Spring tonic
ice cream

1/2 cup half-and-half
3/4 cup sugar
  1 tablespoon unflavored gelatin, softened
     pinch salt

1/2 cup rhubarb sauce
1/2 cup fresh strawberries
1-1/2 cups whipping cream

Step 1

Heat half-and-half in top of double boiler. Add sugar, gelatin, and salt, stirring constantly until dissolved. Cool.

Step 2

Buzz rhubarb sauce, strawberries, and cream in blender until fruit is pureed. Add to cooled mixture. Chill one hour and churn.

This ice cream is so light and springy it fairly dances in your mouth. While we make no miraculous claims for its curative powers for the body, we know it is good for the spirits.

43

Butter almond toffee crème

1/4 cup slivered almonds
   1 tablespoon butter

1-1/2 cups whole milk
   1/2 cup brown sugar
        pinch salt

1-1/2 cups whipping cream
   1 Heath Bar, crushed

Step 1
Brown almonds slightly in butter. Drain on paper towels.

Step 2
Heat milk in top of double boiler. Add sugar and salt, stirring until dissolved. Add nuts and cool.

Step 3
Combine cream and Heath Bar with cooled mixture. Chill two hours and churn.

Some kind of nut

1 cup whole milk
1/2 cup honey
1 teaspoon unflavored gelatin, softened

1/2 cup combination of your favorite nuts. (We like mixing two
   or three of the following: chopped filberts, sunflower seeds,
   pine nuts, chopped brazil nuts, chopped pumpkin seeds,
   chopped cashews, or chopped pecans.)
2 tablespoons butter

1-1/2 cups whipping cream
1 teaspoon vanilla

Step 1
Combine milk, honey, and gelatin in top of double boiler and
heat until gelatin is dissolved.

Step 2
Add nuts and butter to ingredients in double boiler and heat,
stirring constantly, for five minutes. Cool.

Step 3
Combine cream and vanilla with cooled mixture. Chill one
hour and churn.

45

Thanksgiving ice cream

> 1 cup half-and-half
> 3/4 cup canned pumpkin pie mix
> 1/3 cup honey
>   pinch salt
>
> 2 egg yolks
>
> 1 cup whipping cream
> 1/4 cup chopped walnuts
> 1/4 teaspoon cinnamon
> 1/4 teaspoon ginger

Step 1
Combine half-and-half, pie mix, honey, and salt, and heat in top of double boiler.

Step 2
Beat egg yolks until thick and yellow. Add a small amount of warm mixture to yolks. Combine yolks with milk mixture in top of double boiler. Heat, stirring constantly, until slightly thickened. Cool.

Step 3
Combine cream, walnuts, cinnamon, and ginger with cooled mixture. Chill two hours and churn.

The flavors of Thanksgiving are too good to enjoy only once a year. Make this ice cream anytime you want a rich, smooth treat.

Ginger snappy ice cream

1 cup whole milk
1/2 cup sugar
2 teaspoons unflavored gelatin, softened
  pinch salt

2 cups half-and-half
1/4 cup crystallized ginger, minced
1 teaspoon ginger
1/4 cup walnuts

Step 1
Heat milk in top of double boiler. Add sugar, gelatin, and salt, stirring constantly until dissolved. Cool.

Step 2
Combine remaining ingredients with cooled mixture. Chill one hour and churn.

To add a piquantly crunchy texture to this dessert, serve it over a few ginger snap cookies.

Rummy raisin

1/3 cup raisins, chopped
  3 tablespoons rum

1/2 cup half-and-half
  2 teaspoons unflavored gelatin, softened
1/2 cup sugar

1/2 cup whole milk
  2 cups whipping cream
  1 teaspoon rum flavoring

Step 1
Combine raisins and rum, and allow to mellow one hour.

Step 2
Heat half-and-half in top of double boiler. Add sugar and gelatin, stirring constantly until dissolved. Add raisin mixture and heat five minutes, stirring constantly. Cool.

Step 3
Add milk, cream, and rum flavoring to cooled mixture. Chill one hour and churn.

Caramel crunch

---

2 tablespoons butter, melted
1/3 cup sunflower seeds

3/4 cup sugar
2/3 cup half-and-half

2 cups whipping cream
1 tablespoon vanilla

Step 1
Brown sunflower seeds slightly in melted butter over low heat.

Step 2
Melt sugar over low heat in heavy skillet until it begins to burn. Carefully add half-and-half and stir until smooth. Add sunflower seeds and butter. Cool.

Step 3
Add cream and vanilla to cooled mixture. Chill two hours and churn.

Lemon chiffon ice cream

4 egg yolks
2/3 cup sugar

1 cup small curd cottage cheese, blended until smooth
1-1/2 cup half-and-half
1 teaspoon grated lemon peel
2 tablespoons lemon juice
1 teaspoon vanilla

2 egg whites

Step 1
Beat egg yolks until thick and yellow. Continue beating while slowly adding sugar.

Step 2
Combine cottage cheese, half-and-half, lemon peel, lemon juice, and vanilla, and add to egg yolk mixture. Chill two hours.

Step 3
Beat egg whites until stiff peaks form. Fold into chilled mixture and churn.

A childhood favorite of ours, lemon chiffon ice cream combines a creamy, smooth texture with the brightness of lemon. The addition of the cottage cheese in this recipe gives body to the dessert while packing it with protein.

Maui zowie
ice cream

3 egg yolks
1/2 cup sugar

2 cups whipping cream
1 teaspoon vanilla
1/3 cup fresh pineapple, crushed and drained
1/4 cup flaked coconut
2-3 tablespoons macadamia nuts, chopped fine

Step 1

Beat egg yolks until thick and yellow. Continue beating and add sugar slowly.

Step 2

Combine remaining ingredients and add to egg yolk mixture. Chill two hours and churn.

This island masterpiece combines several luscious and exotic flavors and textures. If you substitute honey for the sugar in this recipe, you will get an entirely different, but thoroughly delicious, taste.

51

Mocha
ice cream

2 tablespoons cocoa
2 tablespoons instant coffee crystals
1/2 cup sugar
1/8 teaspoon salt
1/2 cup evaporated milk
2 teaspoons unflavored gelatin, softened

2 cups whipping cream
1 cup half-and-half

Step 1
Mix together cocoa, coffee crystals, sugar, and salt in top of double boiler. Slowly add evaporated milk, stirring constantly to avoid lumps. Heat. Add softened gelatin, stirring until dissolved. Cool.

Step 2
Add cream and half-and-half to cooled mixture. Chill two hours and churn.

Coffee and chocolate lovers, unite! The whole may be greater than the sum of its parts. This simple recipe has a rich chocolate flavor emboldened with the slightly bitter zip of coffee. An after-hours treat for the adults in the family.

Grasshopper ice cream

1/2 cups evaporated milk
  2 teaspoons unflavored gelatin, softened
1/2 cup sugar
1/2 cup green creme de menthe

  2 cups whipping cream
  1 teaspoon vanilla
    green food coloring, if desired

Step 1
Combine milk, gelatin, sugar, and creme de menthe in top of double boiler. Heat, stirring constantly, for ten minutes. Cool.

Step 2
Add cream, vanilla, and food coloring to cooled mixture. Chill one hour and churn.

This is a solid basic ice cream with a mint twist. The liqueur gives it an "R" rating; serve it as a combination dessert and after-dinner drink to friends.

Easy honey pecan ice cream

2 cups whipping cream
1/2 cup evaporated milk
1/2 cup honey
1 tablespoon vanilla

2/3 cup finely chopped pecans
3 tablespoons butter

Step 1
Mix cream, milk, honey, and vanilla, and chill for two hours.

Step 2
Lightly brown pecans in butter. Drain and cool on paper towels. Add to ice cream mixture and churn.

Shoo-fly ice cream

2 tablespoons butter, melted
1/8 teaspoon nutmeg
1 teaspoon cinnamon

1/4 cup unsulphured molasses
1/2 cup brown sugar

1 cup half-and-half
2 cups whipping cream

Step 1
Stir nutmeg and cinnamon in melted butter over boiling water for three minutes.

Step 2
Add molasses and sugar to spices and continue stirring until well blended and sugar is completely dissolved. Cool.

Step 3
Add half-and-half and cream to cooled mixture. Chill two hours and churn.

In Pennsylvania Dutch country, as well as down in the South, Shoo-fly Pie is a favorite. One of your authors, an eighth-generation Southerner, has risked family reprisal to convert an ancient family pie recipe to ice cream. It's different and has a mind of its own—see what you think.

How to make frozen yogurt

Although ice cream has been around for centuries, and so has yogurt, it was only recently that frozen yogurt appeared on the scene. Let's welcome the delicious newcomer with its many qualities. First, it has a zesty lightness and clear, clean taste. It is a healthful food with lots of protein. And, of all things, it is economical in calories, having half to two-thirds the calorie count of ice cream. As a bonus, it is even easier to make than homemade ice cream. Let us see how to make this fine new discovery, then sample some of the recipes from the infinite variety open to us.

Making frozen yogurt is a snap. In general, you follow the same procedures you use to make ice cream: fix a mix and freeze it in your pet kind of machine. Frozen yogurt may even be easier than homemade ice cream because the mixes are easier to prepare. You just cannot go wrong with frozen yogurt; it's easy to fix, good for you, low in calories, and tastes great. There are a few tips that can make your frozen yogurt even better.

First, try using your own yogurt. It is so easy to make yogurt at home that it is hard to see why so many of us continue to pay over twice the price for the store-bought kind. There are many ways to make yogurt; here are four.

59

The fancy way is to buy a yogurt maker. There are several on the market, and they all work about the same way. You bring milk up to a boil, then let it cool back down to a thoroughly warm but not hot temperature. This is a temperature at which you could keep your finger in it for ten to fifteen seconds without being uncomfortable. Then you stir in a few tablespoons of plain yogurt, put the mix in the machine, and leave it alone for a few hours. The yogurt maker keeps the milk mixture at a stable temperature so that the yogurt culture can "yoge" the milk.

We have tested three simple ways to make yogurt. In each case you bring milk to a boil, then let it cool down to the previously mentioned temperature. Mix a few tablespoons of yogurt with a little warm milk, then mix it all together. The next task is to find a way to keep it warm for the six to ten hours it takes to make yogurt.

One way is to pour the mixture into a wide-mouthed vacuum bottle. The bottle will keep the liquid at the same temperature long enough for the culture to turn it into yogurt. Another way is to pour the mix into a bowl, cover it, then set the bowl on a heating pad (turned on High) overnight. The third easy way is to put your mix in a covered bowl in a warm oven. When we make yogurt, we usually make a quart or two in the evening, then let it sit on the heating pad overnight. We then have fresh yogurt the next morning. Generally the longer the yogurt sits, the tarter and thicker it becomes. You will have to vary the time it sits depending on how tart and thick you want it. We like nine to ten hour yogurt best.

Our preference is toward whole milk yogurt when making frozen yogurt. The calorie difference between whole milk and

60

low-fat is not enormous (about 30 calories per cup), and the whole milk kind has a richer, smoother taste and texture to it. If you prefer, though, low-fat and even non-fat yogurt can be used, although you will probably need to use a thickener such as gelatin or beaten egg whites.

We recommend that you use as few sweeteners as possible. The tartness of yogurt is, in our opinion, part of its charm. The natural sweeteners, such as those in fruits, are the best complement to yogurt. We have had great success with raspberries, peaches, strawberries, and pineapple. Once, when possessed with a fruit-less refrigerator and a case of the late-night munchies, we made a fantastic frozen yogurt out of a can of fruit cocktail. If you tire of the fresh fruits available to you in your area, pay a visit to the preserves section of a gourmet store or a well-stocked natural foods store. There you will find many exotic flavors (lingonberries, guava, rose hips, blackberry) that will add zip to your frozen yogurt.

Frozen yogurt recipes

French vanilla frozen yogurt

1/2 cup evaporated milk
  2 teaspoons unflavored gelatin, softened
2/3 cup raw sugar
    pinch salt

  2 egg yolks

  2 cups plain whole milk yogurt
  2 tablespoons vanilla

  2 egg whites

Step 1
Heat evaporated milk in top of double boiler. Add gelatin, sugar, and salt, stirring constantly until dissolved.

Step 2
Beat egg yolks until thick and yellow. Add a small amount of warm mixture to egg yolks. Then slowly add yolks to ingredients in double boiler, stirring constantly. Continue stirring until mixture begins to thicken. Cool.

Step 3
Add yogurt and vanilla to cooled mixture and chill one hour.

Step 4

Beat egg whites until soft peaks form. Gently fold into chilled mixture and churn.

We began the ice cream section with two vanilla recipes, and now let us introduce frozen yogurt in the same way. This recipe makes a smooth, frosty dessert with an undercurrent of incomparably simple vanilla.

Vanilla
frozen yogurt

2 cups plain whole milk yogurt
1/2 cup honey
1 cup evaporated milk
2 tablespoons vanilla

Mix ingredients together. Chill two hours and churn.

This recipe is simplicity itself. Five minutes to make the mix, no cooking, and a clean, brisk taste to reward yourself an hour or two later.

Pineapple orange frozen yogurt

2-1/2 cups plain whole milk yogurt
  2/3 cup raw sugar
  1/3 cup frozen orange juice concentrate
  1/3 cup fresh pineapple bits

Mix ingredients together. Chill two hours and churn.

A tangy treat that mingles the delicate flavors of orange and pineapple. For an even tarter taste, leave out the sweetener entirely.

68

Carob
frozen yogurt

1/2 cup carob powder
1/2 cup water
1/4 cup corn syrup
1/4 cup honey
   1 teaspoon vanilla

2-1/2 cups plain whole milk yogurt

Step 1
Mix carob powder with water in heavy saucepan. Add corn syrup, honey, and vanilla, and heat, stirring constantly, for three minutes. Cool.

Step 2
Add yogurt to carob mixture, and chill two hours. Churn.

The natural foods revolution has brought with it some winning new flavors, among them carob. Try it out to see how you like this recipe in comparison to chocolate ice cream.

Raspberry frozen yogurt

2 cups plain whole milk yogurt
1 cup fresh raspberry puree
1/3 cup honey

Combine ingredients, chill two hours, and churn.

Another five-minute favorite. Buzz up some raspberries in the blender, add yogurt and honey, freeze, and enjoy.

Tangy butterscotch freeze

2/3 cup brown sugar
3 tablespoons butter
  pinch salt

1/4 cup evaporated milk
1 teaspoon unflavored gelatin, softened
2 teaspoons vanilla

2-1/2 cups plain whole milk yogurt

Step 1
Melt butter over low heat. Add brown sugar and salt, stirring constantly until smooth and bubbly.

Step 2
Heat milk in top of double boiler and add gelatin, vanilla, and brown sugar mixture. Heat, stirring constantly, until all ingredients are dissolved. Cool.

Step 3
Blend sugar mixture into yogurt. Chill two hours. Churn.

The smooth, buttery richness of butterscotch combines well with the tongue-titillating tartness of yogurt to create a come-hither taste all its own.

Fresh peach
frozen yogurt

2-1/2 cups plain whole milk yogurt
  1/2 cup raw sugar
  1/3 cup fresh peaches, peeled and chopped
    1 teaspoon vanilla

     Ginger or mace may be added

Mix all ingredients together, chill two hours and churn.

Light, fresh, and creamy, this frozen yogurt is one of our favorites.

Honey-lemon frozen yogurt

2/3 cup honey
2 tablespoons lemon juice
1 teaspoon grated lemon rind
pinch salt

2 cups plain whole milk yogurt

2 egg whites

Step 1
Combine honey, lemon juice, rind, and salt in heavy saucepan over medium heat and stir until well blended. Cool.

Step 2
Mix yogurt together with honey mixture and chill two hours.

Step 3
Beat egg whites until stiff peaks form. Fold gently into yogurt mixture and churn.

Honey and lemon go together beautifully in frozen yogurt. The honey gives the dessert a smooth texture and natural sweetness, while the lemon imparts a bright snap to the taste.

73

Cranapple frozen yogurt

1 cup finely chopped apples
3/4 cup cranberry juice
1/2 cup raw sugar
    pinch salt

2 teaspoons unflavored gelatin, softened

1-1/2 cups plain whole milk yogurt

Step 1
Combine apples, cranberry juice, sugar, and salt in heavy saucepan and bring to boil. Reduce heat and simmer until apples are soft. Beat for one minute with a wooden spoon.

Step 2
Add gelatin to cranberry and apple mixture and heat, stirring constantly, until gelatin is dissolved. Cool.

Step 3
Combine yogurt with cooled mixture and chill one hour. Churn.

Desert oasis frozen yogurt

1/3 cup minced dates
2/3 cup honey

1 tablespoon unflavored gelatin, softened
1/3 cup evaporated milk

2 cups plain whole milk yogurt

Step 1
Mix dates and honey.

Step 2
Heat milk in top of double boiler. Add softened gelatin and date-honey mixture, stirring constantly until smooth. Cool.

Step 3
Combine yogurt with other ingredients. Chill one hour and churn.

75

Spicy apple frozen yogurt

---

   1 cup apple butter
1/3 cup honey
1/4 teaspoon cinnamon
      pinch nutmeg
      pinch ginger
      pinch salt

   2 cups plain whole milk yogurt

Step 1
Combine all ingredients except yogurt. Mix well and allow to stand to blend flavors.

Step 2
Add yogurt to apple butter mixture. Chill two hours and churn.

This is a gourmet frozen yogurt. Although easy to make, the haunting blend of flavors and intriguing texture will satisfy the most discerning palates.

76

Yogurt 'n cheese freeze

1 cup plain whole milk yogurt
1 cup cream style cottage cheese
2/3 cup honey
1 teaspoon lemon juice
3/4 cup fresh fruit, chopped

Combine all ingredients in blender until smooth. Chill two hours and churn.

A high protein powerhouse, this frozen yogurt is full of natural flavors and low in calories. Confirmed calorie-counters can substitute artificial sweetener for some of the honey.

Maple yogurt custard

---

   3 egg yolks
3/4 cup pure maple syrup
       pinch salt

   2 cups plain whole milk yogurt

   2 egg whites

Step 1
Beat egg yolks until thick and yellow. Add syrup and salt, and heat mixture in top of double boiler, stirring constantly, until mixture thickens. Cool.

Step 2
Combine yogurt with egg and maple syrup mixture. Chill two hours.

Step 3
Beat egg whites until stiff. Fold into chilled mixture and churn.

Rhubarb & raisin frozen yogurt

1/2 cup fresh rhubarb, chopped
1/4 cup seedless raisins
1/3 cup honey
1/2 cup water

2 cups plain whole milk yogurt
1 teaspoon vanilla extract

Step 1
Bring rhubarb, raisins, honey, and water to boil in heavy saucepan. Lower heat and simmer twenty to thirty minutes. Cool.

Step 2
Combine yogurt and vanilla extract with rhubarb and raisin sauce. Chill two hours and churn.

79

Chocolate & nut chip frozen yogurt

2/3 cup raw sugar
1/2 cup whole milk

1/2 cup crushed chocolate chips
1/3 cup chopped walnuts or pecans
  2 cups plain whole milk yogurt
  1 tablespoon vanilla extract

Step 1
Stir milk and sugar together until sugar is completely dissolved.

Step 2
Add remaining ingredients to sugar mixture and combine thoroughly. Chill two hours and churn.

80

Blueberry frozen yogurt

1 cup fresh blueberries, crushed
1/2 cup powdered sugar
1 teaspoon grated lemon rind

2-1/2 cups plain whole milk yogurt

Step 1
Combine crushed blueberries, sugar, and lemon rind. Allow to stand thirty minutes.

Step 2
Add yogurt to blueberry mixture. Chill two hours and churn.

Cinnamon stick— yogurt freeze

2 sticks cinnamon candy, crushed
1/2 cup whole milk
1 tablespoon unflavored gelatin, softened

2-1/2 cups plain whole milk yogurt
1 teaspoon vanilla extract
1/4 teaspoon ground cinnamon

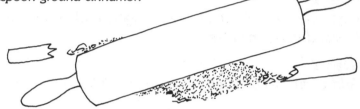

Step 1
Combine candy, milk, and gelatin in top of double boiler. Heat, stirring constantly, for five minutes. Cool.

Step 2
Combine yogurt, vanilla extract, and cinnamon with cooled candy mixture. Chill one hour and churn.

Sherbets and ices

It's handy to have some sherbet and ice recipes on hand for those times when you are looking for a delicious dessert with the lightest possible touch. Sherbets and ices can be made with very simple ingredients or with a devilish complexity of flavors. Either way they are light, low in calories, and hard to resist.

Although you will want to make sherbets the same way you make ice cream and frozen yogurt, you need not churn-freeze ices. It is easier to still-freeze the mixture, then pulverize it in your blender. You can then pop it back in the freezer for a few minutes to set to the consistency you like it. Ices, unlike ice cream and frozen yogurt, do not seem to suffer from still-freezing.

87

Peach sherbet

2 cups peaches, peeled and pitted
1/2 cup honey
1 tablespoon lemon juice

1 cup skim milk or whole milk
1/3 cup sugar
2 teaspoons unflavored gelatin, softened
1/4 teaspoon almond extract

Step 1
Puree peaches in blender. Add honey and lemon juice while continuing to blend.

Step 2
Heat milk in top of double boiler. Add sugar, gelatin, and almond extract. Continue heating, stirring constantly until sugar and gelatin are dissolved. Combine with pureed peaches and chill one hour. Churn.

A masterpiece of lightness, this recipe makes a quart of the most refreshing dessert you'll ever taste. And, as with many of the sherbets and ices, the calorie count is happily low.

88

Currant sherbet

1 cup dried currants
1 cup water

2 cups skim milk
1/2 cup honey
2 teaspoons unflavored gelatin, softened
  pinch salt

1 egg white

Step 1
Combine currants and water and allow to stand until currants are plumped. Strain.

Step 2
Heat milk in top of double boiler. Add honey, gelatin, and salt, stirring constantly until dissolved. Add currants and cook, stirring constantly, until smooth. Chill one hour.

Step 3
Beat egg whites until stiff peaks form. Fold into chilled mixture and churn.

Currants are great for baking, but who would think of putting them in sherbet? We did it, and it worked. For a different slant, add a dash of rum flavoring.

Mint julep sherbet

2 cups whole or skim milk
1 cup sugar
1/2 cup bourbon
2 tablespoons fresh mint leaves

1/2 cup water

2 egg whites

Step 1
Heat milk in top of double boiler. Add sugar, bourbon, and mint leaves. Simmer, stirring constantly, for five minutes. Strain into bowl to remove mint leaves.

Step 2
Add water to milk mixture and chill two hours.

Step 3
Beat egg whites until soft peaks form. Fold into chilled mixture and churn.

Chilling lightness with a bold bourbon undercurrent, this sherbet is for those summer evenings when you are sitting on the veranda reminiscing about the way things used to be.

90

Waldorf sherbet

1 cup apples, peeled, cored, and chopped
1 cup water
1 stick cinnamon

   1 cup whole or skim milk
2/3 cup honey
   2 teaspoons unflavored gelatin, softened
     pinch salt

1/3 cup finely chopped apples
1/4 cup finely chopped walnuts

Step 1

Bring cup of apples, water, and cinnamon to a boil in a heavy saucepan. Reduce heat and simmer thirty minutes. Remove cinnamon stick. Cool and puree in blender or food mill.

Step 2

Heat milk in top of double boiler. Add honey, gelatin, and salt and heat, stirring constantly, until dissolved. Cool and combine with apple puree. Chill one hour.

Step 3

Add finely chopped apples and walnuts to chilled mix and churn.

When we were growing up, Waldorf Salad was a family favorite, served with a fancy Sunday dinner. Here the flavors are combined into a light but satisfying dessert.

Traditional orange sherbet

1-1/2 cups whole milk
  3/4 cup sugar
    2 teaspoons unflavored gelatin, softened

    2 cups freshly squeezed orange juice
    2 tablespoons grated orange rind
    1 tablespoon lemon juice

    2 egg whites

Step 1
Heat milk in top of double boiler. Add sugar and gelatin, stirring constantly until dissolved. Cool.

Step 2
Combine orange juice, rind, and lemon juice with milk mixture. Chill one hour.

Step 3
Beat egg whites until soft peaks form. Fold into orange juice mixture and churn.

This is your basic orange sherbet, but with a freshness and lightness you will not find in the store-bought version.

Banana sherbet

---

  2 cups whole milk
1/2 cup sugar
1/4 cup corn syrup

  1 ripe or overripe banana
  2 tablespoons lemon juice
3/4 cup water

  2 egg whites

Step 1
Heat milk in top of double boiler. Add sugar and syrup, and continue to heat, stirring constantly, for five minutes. Cool.

Step 2
Mash banana with lemon juice and stir in water. Combine with milk mixture. Chill two hours.

Step 3
Beat egg whites until stiff peaks form. Fold into chilled mixture and churn.

Sunny lemon sherbet

2-1/2 cups whole milk
    1 cup sugar
    2 tablespoons unflavored gelatin, softened

  1/2 cup freshly squeezed lemon juice
    2 tablespoons grated lemon rind
  1/2 cup chopped or coarsely ground sunflower seeds
  2-3 drops yellow food coloring, if desired

Step 1
Heat milk in top of double boiler. Add sugar and gelatin, stirring constantly until dissolved. Chill one hour.

Step 2
Add remaining ingredients to chilled mixture. Churn immediately.

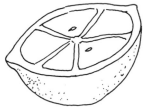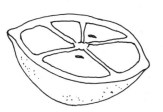

Apricot sherbet

6 oz. dried apricots
2 cups water
2 tablespoons lemon juice

2 cups milk
3/4 cups sugar
pinch salt

2 egg whites

Step 1
Combine apricots, water, and lemon juice in heavy saucepan; bring to boil. Reduce heat and simmer fifteen to twenty minutes. Cool. Buzz mixture in blender until pureed.

Step 2
Heat milk in top of double boiler. Add sugar and salt, stirring constantly until dissolved. Cool and combine with pureed apricots. Chill two hours.

Step 3
Beat egg whites until stiff peaks form. Fold into chilled mixture and churn.

Cranberry sherbet

1-1/2 cups whole milk
   2 teaspoons unflavored gelatin, softened
  1/4 cup sugar

1-1/2 cups cranberry sauce
   2 tablespoons lemon juice
   2 tablespoons frozen orange juice concentrate

Step 1
Heat milk in top of double boiler. Add sugar and gelatin, stirring constantly until dissolved. Cool.

Step 2
Buzz cranberry sauce, lemon juice, and orange juice concentrate in blender until cranberry pieces are minced. Stir into milk mixture. Chill one hour and churn.

Cranberry sauce

2 cups water
2 cups whole fresh cranberries
2 cups sugar

Combine in large saucepan. Bring to boil. Reduce heat and simmer until cranberries pop and mixture thickens. Cool.

Grape sherbet

1 cup whole milk
1/4 cup sugar
   pinch salt

1 6-oz. can frozen grape juice concentrate
1 cup whole milk

2 egg whites

Step 1
Heat milk in top of double boiler. Add sugar and salt, stirring constantly until dissolved. Cool.

Step 2
Add concentrate and milk to cooled mixture and chill two hours.

Step 3
Beat egg whites until soft peaks form and gently fold into grape juice mixture. Churn.

Pineapple-tangerine ice

2 cups fresh pineapple, chopped
1 6-oz. can frozen concentrated tangerine juice
1/4 cup sugar
1 cup water

Combine all ingredients in blender until pureed. Chill two hours and churn.

Birthday party ice

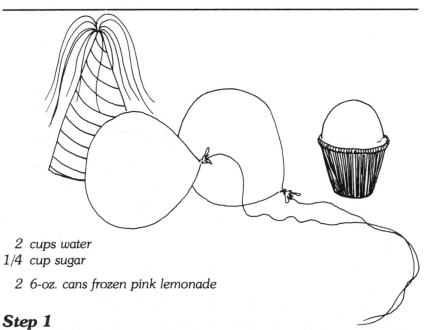

2 cups water
1/4 cup sugar
2 6-oz. cans frozen pink lemonade

Step 1
Combine water and sugar in top of double boiler. Heat, stirring constantly, for five minutes.

Step 2
Add lemonade to above mixture and chill two hours. Churn or still-freeze.

Super iced tea

3 cups strong orange-spice tea, strained
  1/2 cup honey
    2 tablespoons lemon juice
    1 teaspoon grated orange peel

Combine ingredients in top of double boiler, stirring constantly until honey is dissolved. Chill two hours, churn or still-freeze.

100

May
ice

1-1/2 cups dry white wine
  3/4 cup sugar

    2 cups fresh strawberries

Step 1
Bring wine and sugar to boil in heavy saucepan. Reduce heat and simmer five minutes, stirring constantly.

Step 2
Puree strawberries and add to wine mixture. Chill two hours, churn or still-freeze.

Frozen May wine makes a lovely springtime treat for the family. Since the alcohol evaporates when the wine is heated, even the children can enjoy this festive treat.

101

Nectarine ice

2 cups well ripened nectarines, peeled and pitted
1/2 cup orange juice

1 cup water
1/2 cup honey
1/4 teaspoon almond extract

Step 1
Combine nectarines and orange juice in blender and puree.

Step 2
Heat water, honey, and almond extract in double boiler, stirring constantly for five minutes. Add to nectarine puree and chill two hours. Churn or still-freeze.

Tangy pear ice

2 cups canned pears, drained
1/2 cup water

1 cup grapefruit juice
1/3 cup sugar

Step 1
Combine pears and water in blender and puree.

Step 2
Mix juice and sugar until sugar is dissolved. Add to pear puree and chill two hours. Churn or still-freeze.

Fire & ice

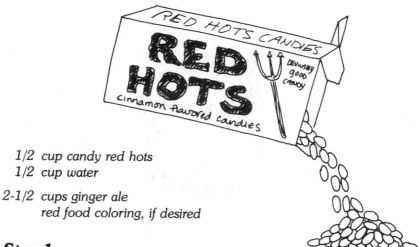

1/2 cup candy red hots
1/2 cup water

2-1/2 cups ginger ale
    red food coloring, if desired

Step 1
Heat candy and water in top of double boiler until candy is dissolved and mixture syrupy.

Step 2
Combine ginger ale and coloring with candy mixture and chill one hour. Churn or still-freeze.

Children's favorite

2-1/2 cans soda pop (7-Up, Root Beer, Orange, Cola, etc.)
  1/4 cup sugar
  2-3 drops food coloring, as desired

Combine ingredients and stir until sugar is completely dissolved. Chill two hours and churn.

Icy watermelon cooler

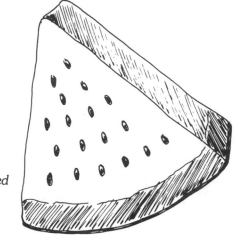

3/4 cup water
1/2 cup sugar

3 cups watermelon, seeded
1 tablespoon lemon juice

Step 1
Combine water and sugar in heavy saucepan and simmer five minutes, stirring constantly.

Step 2
Puree watermelon with lemon juice in blender. Add to sugar syrup and chill two hours. Churn or still-freeze.

106

Rhubarb ice

2 cups water
1/2 cup honey
1 cup rhubarb sauce

Heat and stir honey and water until combined. Add sauce to honey-water mixture. Chill two hours, churn or still-freeze.

107

For the adventurous: breakfast ice creams and frozen first courses

Bored with bran flakes for breakfast? Tired of the old gazpacho grind? Sick of vitiated vichysoisse? Then it is clear that you need to venture out into the cold: into the world of breakfast ice creams and frozen first courses. If somewhere inside you is a gourmet cook trying to get out, you won't rest easy until you have whipped up a tomato aspic sherbet or a protein-packed breakfast ice cream.

For the adventurous, here is a starter collection of exotic eatables that will give you something to stand up and churn about.

111

Yogurt-granola breakfast

2 cups plain whole milk yogurt
1 cup crunchy granola
2/3 cup honey
2 tablespoons high protein powder

Mix ingredients together and chill two hours. Churn.

It is easy to get stuck in a breakfast rut, but with a bit of imagination you can remake that early meal into an exciting affair. Here is a frozen yogurt that meets all the requirements of a good breakfast. It is loaded with protein and has a satisfying crunch to it.

Honey date ice cream

---

  2 cups half-and-half
  1 cup instant non-fat dry milk
  2 tablespoons brewer's yeast
  1 egg
2/3 cup honey
  1 teaspoon vanilla

1/3 cup chopped dates
1/3 cup grapenuts cereal

Step 1

Combine half-and-half, milk, yeast, egg, honey, and vanilla in blender and mix until smooth.

Step 2

Add dates and cereal to this mixture and chill two hours. Churn.

A bowl of ice cream for breakfast is beyond even an ice cream lover's wildest dreams. But why not? Churned to a soft consistency and full of nutritious things, ice cream is a nearly perfect starter for the day. Give it a try.

Protein-packed day starter

2 cups whipping cream
1/2 cup non-fat dry milk (not instant)
2 eggs
1/4 cup ground almonds
1/4 cup ground sunflower seeds
1/4 cup ground sesame
1/2 cup honey
2 tablespoons high protein powder

1/2 cup chopped pecans

Step 1
Combine all ingredients except pecans in blender and mix until smooth.

Step 2
Add pecans to the mixture, chill two hours. Churn.

Hi-vitamin eye opener

1 cup orange juice
2 teaspoons unflavored gelatin, softened
1/3 cup honey

1 cup instant non-fat dry milk
1 cup whole milk yogurt

1 cup fresh or fresh-frozen strawberries

Step 1
Heat juice in top of double boiler. Add gelatin and honey, stirring until gelatin is dissolved. Cool slightly.

Step 2
Mix dry milk and yogurt together. Add juice mixture cooked.

Step 3
Puree strawberries in blender and add to cooled ingredients. Chill one hour and churn.

115

Banana breakfast

3 tablespoons carob powder
1/2 cup non-fat dry milk
1/2 cup raw sugar
    pinch salt
2 cups half-and-half

2 egg yolks

1 ripe banana
1 tablespoon lemon juice
1/4 cup sesame seeds

2 egg whites

Step 1

Mix carob powder, dry milk, sugar, and salt in top of double boiler. Slowly add half-and-half, stirring until smooth. Heat, stirring constantly, until sugar mixture is dissolved.

Step 2

Beat egg yolks until frothy. Add a small amount of warm mixture to the beaten eggs. Slowly combine eggs with warm mixture, stirring constantly until mixture begins to thicken. Cool.

116

Step 3
Mash banana with lemon juice and stir in sesame seeds. Combine with egg-and-milk mixture and chill.

Step 4
Beat egg whites until stiff peaks form. Fold into chilled mixture and churn.

If you would like more of the taste of banana to come through, leave out the carob and substitute a teaspoon of vanilla.

Guacamole sherbet

2 ripe avocados, peeled and mashed
2 tablespoons lemon juice
3 tablespoons green onion, minced
1 teaspoon salt
1/4 teaspoon chili powder

1 cup whole milk
1 cup water

2 egg whites

Step 1
Combine avocados, lemon juice, onion, salt, and chili powder, and mix well.

Step 2
Add milk and water to avocado mixture in blender and puree. Chill two hours.

Step 3
Beat egg whites until soft peaks form. Fold into chilled mixture and churn.

Tomato aspic sherbet

1   12 ounce can peeled stewed tomatoes
2   tablespoons chopped onion
1   stalk celery with leaves
1   tablespoon lemon juice
2   teaspoons unflavored gelatin, softened
1   teaspoon salt
1/4 teaspoon pepper

Combine ingredients in heavy saucepan and bring to boil. Reduce heat and simmer thirty minutes. Cool and puree in blender. Add water as needed to make three cups of puree. Chill one hour and churn.

Gazpacho sherbet

1 cup tomato juice
1 cup cucumber, peeled and diced
1/4 cup chopped green pepper
3 tablespoons chopped onion
2 tablespoons chopped chives
2 tablespoons lemon juice
1/2 teaspoon salt
1/4 teaspoon paprika
1/4 teaspoon garlic powder

1/2 cup whole milk

2 egg whites

Step 1
Combine all ingredients except milk and egg whites in blender and puree.

Step 2
Add milk to pureed ingredients and chill two hours.

Step 3
Beat egg whites until stiff peaks form. Fold into chilled mixture and churn.

Vichyssoise ice cream

1 leek, thinly sliced
2 tablespoons butter

1 cup chicken broth
1 medium potato, chopped
2 teaspoons unflavored gelatin, softened
1 teaspoon salt

1-1/2 cups whipping cream
2 tablespoons chopped chives

Step 1
Gently sauté leek in butter.

Step 2
Add leek to potato, salt, gelatin, and chicken broth in heavy saucepan. Simmer thirty minutes. Cool slightly and purée in blender.

Step 3
Add cream and chives to potato mixture and chill one hour. Churn.

121